AF447507

THE SECRET

AND POWER

OF

PSALM

91

Tella Olayeri
+2348023583168

All rights reserved. No part of this publication may be reproduced, stored in a retrieval system or transmitted in any form or by any means electronics, mechanical, photocopying, recording, or otherwise, without the prior written permission of the publisher, in accordance with the provisions of the copyright Act.

Any person who does any unauthorized act in relation to this publication may be liable to criminal prosecution and civil claims for damages. It is protected under the copyright laws.

Published By:

GOD'S LINK VENTURES

Email <u>tellaolayeri@gmail.com</u>

Website <u>www.tellaolayeri.com</u>

Blog <u>www.tellaolayeri.com/blog</u>

US Contact
Ruth Jack
14 Milewood Road
Verbank
N.Y.12585
U.S.A. +19176428989

All texts, calls, letters, testimonies and enquiries are welcome.

CONNECT WITH US

FACEBOOK

(Like and follow our page)

https://web.facebook.com/tellaolayeri/

(Join our Facebook Group)

Do you want your dream interpreted, do you need powerful morning and night prayers that command breakthrough, healing and favour.

Join my Facebook group today and receive testimony.

https://web.facebook.com/groups/tellaolayeri

INSTAGRAM

https://www.instagram.com/tellaolayeri/

TWITTER

https://twitter.com/tellaolayeri

APPRECIATION

I give special appreciation to my wife **MRS NGOZI OLAYERI** for her assistance in ensuring that this book is published and our children that play around us to encourage us day and night.

Also, this manuscript wouldn't have seen the light of the day, if not for the spiritual encouragement I gathered from my father in the Lord, **Dr. D.K. OLUKOYA** who served as spiritual mirror that brightens my hope to explore my calling (Evangelism).

We shall all reap our blessings in heaven but the battle to make heaven is not over, until it is won.

PREFACE

Psalm 91 is a unique chapter in the books of the Psalms. This book makes us know God calling us into deeper fellowship with him. We see God talking to us about the Holy Spirit and showing us how to live a victorious life.

It is erroneously believed, Psalm 91 is design to be recited or confessed as a protection scripture. It goes far and wide than this. It is intended to cover every sphere of life. It is a chapter of the Psalms that increases faith, fearlessness, confidence, prayerfulness, and as, a storm breaker, barrier breaker and yoke breaker. It is a book that lights up your altar of prayer.

The author is here to give deep explanation and usefulness of this chapter. He exposes the hidden message of Psalm 91 and encourages you to pray and be a prayer warrior in the war room of fire.

I advise you first read all through and later dedicate each day for each chapter of the book for deep and better understanding. For easy consumption the book is divided into seven chapters, meaning that, each chapter can be dedicated to a day in the week. Meditate on the Word and pray the prayer there in. I encourage you to know the sixteen verses of the chapter off hand.

Pick any day of your choice, fast and pray and be enlisted in the secret place of the Most High. You can do this on a monthly basis depending on your schedule of work. You can pray with it starting from first week of the month or any other day convenient for you. Ensure you read through the first time you buy it to familiarize yourself with it. Thereafter, you can pick a day to start and pray through the seven chapters in seven days.

You will have every reason to thank God after using this book. May God bless you, as you buy and use it. Amen

GOOD NEWS!!!

My audiobook is now available, to get one visit **audible**.

If you are reading from my paperback visit **acx.com** and search **"Tella Olayeri."**

Brethren, to be loaded and reloaded visit: *amazon.com/author/tellaolayeri* for a full spiritual sojourn for my books.

Thanks.

PREVIOUS PUBLICATIONS OF THE AUTHOR

Before we proceed, I'd like to say thank you for downloading this book. I believe the information in it will bless your life greatly. Please find below other books that God has empowered me write. They are meant to be a blessing to your life and family

1. .100% CONFESSIONS and PROPHECIES to Locate Helpers and helpers to locate you
2. 1000 Prayer Points for Children Breakthrough
3. 1010 (One Thousand and Ten) DREAMS and Interpretations
4. 2000 Dangerous Prayer for First Born
5. 365 DREAMS and INTERPRETATIONS
6. 430 Prayers to Cancel Bad Dreams and Overcome Witchcraft Powers part one (DREAMS AND YOU Book 1)
7. 430 Prayers to Claim Good Dreams and Overcome Witchcraft Powers part two (DREAMS AND YOU Book 2)
8. 630 Acidic Prayers: With Missile Prayer for Speedy Breakthrough, Healing and Deliverance
9. 650 DREAMS AND INTERPRETATIONS

94. <u>Warfare Prayer Against Satanic Dream</u>

See all at: <u>amazon.com/author/tellaolayeri</u>

Table of Contents

FREE BOOKS

We must not fold arms in the midst of battle. The life is battle itself. We need to pray and cancel decisions of darkness against us. We are born to win not to lose. Many times we lose out because we don't know how to pray or go about challenges we face.

Also, you must know how to claim and retain what God gives you, called destiny. You must not be robbed!

Brethren, your case is not close until you decide to close it. Don't give up, fight on in faith, you are born to win. Be violent in prayer. The degree of your violence in prayer determines the victory that awaits you. It is time you count spoils not loss, triumph not defeat.

I have some free books for you to put fire to your prayer zeal. Pick them and inform others. Try and share your experience with five to ten people. You may be the one God sent. Don't leave them outside prayer war room.

Be your brother/sister keeper. Good-luck

Click Here to Download

CHAPTER 1

POWER TO DWELL IN THE SECRET PLACE OF GOD

"He that dwelleth in the secret place of the most High shall abide under the shadow of the Almighty. I will say of the LORD, He is my refuge and my fortress: my God; in him will I trust" Psalm 91:1-2

The first verse of Psalm 91 is like a rule. It says, dwell in the secret place of the most High and be protected under the shadow of the Most High God. This promise is a promise to those who are close to God and not church goer. You can sleep in the church, be there early, pay tithe, pay offering, be a member of a group in the church, participate in church activities etc. but if you don't dwell in the secret place of the most High, you miss it all! To dwell in the secret place of God means to be close to God, marry yourself to Him, seek Him, live with Him, be Born Again, seek His face all the time, regard Him as your personal Lord and savior and be a righteous man or woman. You need these spiritual ingredients to qualify as someone under his shadow. These are ingredients that qualify you to know heavenly secret. When you live a righteous life, God will open your eyes to see deep things of heaven. The book of revelation was written by one of the Apostles of Jesus, by name John the Beloved. God opened his inner eyes to see what he wouldn't imagine in the first place. Till today, what he wrote is relevant. Why is this so?, because he dwell in the secret place of the Most High.

Psalm 91 verse 1 is a foundational power to those who seeks the face of God. It is an instruction verse that leads to other verses of the chapter. You must learn what God's secret place is and find out how to live there to dominate and be victorious.

The book of Psalm 91 was dedicated to Moses the man God sent as a deliverer of the children of Isra el. Moses was in the center picture of Israel's history. He was close to God than any other leader of Israel. The background of Psalm 91 can be traced to Moses closeness to God. This is more reason Jewish tradition ascribe Psalm 91 to him. He felt the presence of God many times and knows its worth. This may have made him start Psalm 91 with, ***"He that dwelleth in the secret place of the most High shall abide under the shadow of the Almighty"***.

The background of Moses presence can be traced to, one when God appeared to him in the tent. ***"And it came to pass, as Moss entered into the tabernacle, the cloudy pillar descended, and stood at the door of the tabernacle, and the Lord talked with Moses" Exodus 33:9*** His experience may have led him to write Psalm 91 starting with the secret place and shadow of God

The second experience was when Moses went to meet God at Mount Sinai. He was on the mountain for 40 days and 40 nights. This must have made him understand the importance of knowing God closely being under his shadow and protection. He went again after he broke the first Ten Commandments tablet in anger. He spent another 40 days and 40 nights. All sums up to 80 days and 80 nights with God!. You can't visit a place for 80 days and 80 nights without knowing the importance of the place.

Another book of thought or tradition suggests, Moses composed this verse while he was ascending into the cloud hovering over Mount Sinai, at which time he recited these word as protection from the angels of destruction.

Verse one tells us that God has a secret place for his own, and a place to live in; the habitation and the home of man. It represents the most central chamber of God that inhabits the righteous, etc. with complete security. During the time of Jesus, Peter, James and John occupy better place in his heart. He always calls them to follow him to pray and they are always with him when he goes to the mount to pray. They represent the inner circle of Jesus. They know the secret of the secret place of Jesus. No wonder Peter led, John saw in the book of Revelation.

The secret place empowers one and makes him bold to face and humiliate Satan. It is an inner sanctuary power and mercy-seat of God where deep secret is revealed. This is the reason you must strive hard to be in the secret place of God.

It is in the secret place, you abide under the shadow of the Almighty. The shadow means you are close to God. If you are not close to something or someone, you can't be under its/his shadow. Shadow here means protection. If you walk under the heat of sun or work in the farm and you need rest, you go under the shade of a tree. If a child walks with his parent, he walks under the shadow of his parent. Shadow gives him protection from heat. If there is danger, his father equally gives him protection.

The name of God gives confidence and makes the writer look at it same way. Safety is at hand by saying He is my refuge and my fortress. It is when you live in a place under the roof of a person you will know how secured is the place. With confidence, the writer says there is refuge in the Lord because his abode is a fortress of power with confidence for those who dwell in it. Hence, there is no room for fear or panic under Gods shadow, because the shadow means refuge of unparalleled place, superlative fortress. In a fortress, no storm comes near you, no arrow fired at you comes close to you; no gun shot comes close to you because wall of protection in the form of shadow gives you protection from attack. Suddenly, you are arrow proof, flood proof, storm proof, fire proof and tempest proof against attacks of the enemy.

Based on protection you have under God, you develop faith in him and trust. Your relationship with God is super and undeniable. Comfort under him is unchallengeable. You boast of comfort because Satan cannot come close to you. No suspicion in horizon, testimonies abound here and there, laughter and joy is the order of the day, and you sing your songs and dance your dance to the glory of the Most High.

The book tells us, there is a secret place the Almighty lives, abide and stay. The place is secret because He is the one that knows all about the place. The place was created before Adam and Eve were created and men and women were born. Secret place is secret. If you keep something in your house or room and hide it that place you keep it, is secret. I can't enter your room and point at where you keep it. That place is secret to me, but known to you. God knows all nooks and cranny of the secret place, but men don't. If you don't do his will, you can't enter His secret place.

But then, there is a condition attach to it. He that dwells in the secret place must dwell under the shadow of the Almighty. The shadow gives protection. You don't jump or walk into the secret place unless you know God, do his will and allowed. The first rule is you shall be under his shadow, so that you won't make mistake, but given direction and protected. God is the owner of the secret place, He knows all about the place. The shadow of the Almighty gives protection, it is a shadow of refuge, it makes you fearless. It qualifies you as child of God. A child of God will be close to God, and abide under his shadow.

When you are close to God, it means you do his wish, you run from sin, and seek his face. You cannot be under the shadow of God if you turn your back at Him, which means you do not invite his protective hands upon you. Thus, you swim away in the ocean of darkness, ocean of failure and ocean of loss.

Verse 2 of Psalm 91 says, ***"I will say of the LORD, He is my refuge and my fortress; my God; in him will I trust".*** If you look at this verse very well, you will observe the name LORD is in capital letter not small letter of "Lord" but "LORD". The word LORD appeared first in the book of Genesis chapter 2 verse 4. ***"---When the LORD God made the earth and the heavens"*** This account is the summary of creation. It tells us that God is Almighty, and so, you can only dwell under the shadow of the Almighty and all powerful God. It is only in special occasion the word LORD is used. To conclude creation wasn't a small thing, no wonder God was called LORD.

The Psalmist personalized it, that God is my refuge and my fortress. This means, it is God you can run to for protection or refuge; fortress, or protection and safety etc. the fortress shows it is where God lives; his stronghold. When in His fortress, enemy cannot enter or subdue you. It is a fortress that is powerful, it is a fortress surrounded by fire; it is a holy fortress. It is a fortress of safety. Any power that stubbornly comes close to this fortress, fire shall burn it to ashes. It is this fortress of refuge we can call heavenly palace of peace.

The question is, who is this Most High; the Almighty, the LORD and God mentioned in verse 1 and 2 of this Psalm? They are names of God in character.

1. The Almighty- He is the **Elshadai** which means very powerful. When you are under the control of someone who is very powerful, you will be fearless. If you are with the Almighty you will be happy that God is with you, you will have the conviction that you are save, protected and victorious because the Almighty is there for you. When the Philistines waged war against Israel, Goliath was the almighty of the

Philistines. He roared, talk and boast, no Israel dared him, until David silenced him. If Goliath is feared this way, how will the Almighty be? This means if you are under his shadow Satan will flee.

2. The Most High-**Elyon.** It suggests a Supreme monarch, one who is elevated above all things. The name suggests God's majesty, sovereignty and pre-eminence.

3. The Lord-**Yahweh**. It is personal name for God, revealed to Moses at the burning bush. It suggests God who seeks us to know Him on a deep personal level. It means the all-powerful, divine ruler of all things. He is a God who knows every hair on our heads, every joy and fear in our hearts. He knows all.

4. My God-**Elohim.** It means one who is first or the creator. The Psalmist suggests here the God who he trusts is the same God who created all things, the first and the last, and the God who is forever faithful to His creation.

PRAYER POINTS

1. I shall dwell in the shelter of the Most High in the name of Jesus.

2. Shadow of God, give me protection in the name of Jesus.

3. O Lord, give me divine protection, in the name of Jesus.

4. Any strange power assign to direct my step elsewhere, fail in the name of Jesus.

5. The Lord is my refuge, I shall not die, in the name of Jesus.

6. I trust in the Lord, He shall answer me, in the name of Jesus.

7. Where my God dwells, there I shall be in the name of Jesus.

8. I shall not be a stranger in the house of God, in the name of Jesus.

9. O Lord, empower me to know and understand what is hidden to me in the spirit, in the name of Jesus.

10. I shall not deep hands into sin anymore, in the name of Jesus.

11. O Lord, build my spirit life to discourage attack of the enemy in the name of Jesus.

12. I shall not deep hands into sins anymore, in the name of Jesus.

13. I shall not fear, the Lord is with me, in the name of Jesus.

14. Every barrier standing between me and God break in the name of Jesus.

15. My family tree shall not be cut down in the name of Jesus.

16. I shall not abide in or swim in ocean of failure, in the name of Jesus.

17. I pray, I shall be on the same page with God as his child, in the name of Jesus.

18. O Lord, you are Elshadai, the powerful God, clear every enemy of my soul away, in the name of Jesus.

19. Failure shall not be my portion, in the name of Jesus.

20. Every seed of fear planted in the garden of my life, wither, in the name of Jesus.

21. Every Goliath dedicated against my family, expire, in the name of Jesus.

22. Every power that challenge my existence, expire, in the name of Jesus.

23. Every creation of God obey my voice, so that I may grow, in the name of Jesus.

24. Power drawing me back from God, expire, in the name of Jesus.

25. O Lord, you are my personal Lord and Savior, safe me today in the name of Jesus.

26. O Lord, open my eyes to see deep things of heaven, in the name of Jesus.

27. O Lord, plant seed of relevance in my life, in the name of Jesus.

28. I shall dwell in the central chamber of God, in the name of Jesus.

29. Lord Jesus, let me occupy better place in your heart in the name of Jesus.

30. O Lord, be my fortress where I shall dwell, in the name of Jesus.

31. My faith in God, multiply and improve my destiny in the name of Jesus.

32. I shall sing my song and dance my dance to the glory of God, in Jesus name.

33. Spirit to run from sin, fall upon me, in the name of Jesus.

34. O Lord, I invite your protective hands upon me, lay it on my head, in the name of Jesus.

35. O Lord, I seek your face answer me and protect me, in the name of Jesus.

36. O Lord, surround me with heavenly fire against the wicked ones, in the name of Jesus.

37. O Lord, let me reign with your kingdom.

38. Power to reap good things of life; locate me by fire in the name of Jesus.

CHAPTER 2

POWER OF DELIVERANCE

"Surely he shall deliver thee from the snare of the fowler, and from the noisome pestilence. He shall cover thee with his feathers, and under his wings shalt thou trust: his truth shall be thy shield and buckler." Psalm 91:3-4

The earlier verse in the chapter is the forerunner of verse 3-4. These two verses confirm the experience and expectations built in verses 1 and 2. Here the Psalmist describes specific ways God protects and cares for His people. The first phase of deliverance is; I shall deliver thee from the snare of the fowler and from the noisome pestilence.

Who is a fowler? A Fowler is one who snares birds. He is a professional bird catcher. Birds are snared before they can be caught. The fowler supposes to mean someone who catches bird of prey for domestic use. In the spirit, a fowler here means powers that snare one into captivity, to kill or to captivate him. Imagine you are captivated or simply put in prison for 10 years or more, you may be useless to yourself for life even after you gain freedom. There are people who are in spiritual prison of life for more than 30 years without knowing. Such person walks about, goes to work but won't be able to account for his income. If he is a businessman, he will always count losses year in year out because he is a prisoner in the spirit. Many prisoners are useless to themselves after they are released.

In this verse, the fowler is the bait man. The bait he uses includes stealing, lust, smoking, drunkenness and telling lies. Any person whose bait is opposite sex will be imprisoned by it. He goes into fornication and adultery. He wastes money on this and find it difficult to retrace his steps to good life. If the bait is alcohol, such person will lavish his money in hotels and beer parlors. He won't relax until every penny or cent spent he has on alcohol and women. Most of them support it with cigarette, thereby becomes chain smokers. The end of it all is bad health. Their health deteriorates and bad. Here, they spend all savings in hospital and eventually die suddenly. This is the position of people snared and captured by fowler. To be a victim of fowler is dangerous. Since you are captured in the spirit, you are vulnerable to stagnation, short life, poverty, agony, sorrow, bad health etc. This is the reason the Psalmist says the Lord shall deliver you from the fowler and the noisome pestilence.

People are bait in the hands of fowler through sin and are caged spiritually in chain. It is bad to be a victim of fowler. No wonder David wrote, ***"We have escaped like a bird out of the fowlers snare; the snare has been broken, and we have escaped." Psalm 124:7.*** They are happy when they escaped. Fowler is bad, so is pestilence. When pestilence attack a source, income is eaten up or destroyed. It is said the pestilence is noisome and deadly. Pestilence is plague that destroys. When it comes like locust it destroys plants and eats up leaves of plantation; it sinks life. It is power of nakedness and shame. At the end of the day, it can lead to distress, suicide, and or, untimely death. All these are what God says he will deliver you. This is not what anyone bargains for, because it can bring you from mountain top to the valley.

The noisome pestilence is deadly, known for destruction and emptiness. It empties barns (wealth), destroy crops (handwork) and wages (harvest). They are noisome because they come in groups like locust. They eat up all they see and meet. They feast on wealth and empty destiny. They are wicked, cruel, and emptier in the spirit. Pests eat and are not satisfied. As they eat, so they shit making them unsatisfied. They emptied whatever they feed on. These are powers the Lord shall deliver you from today, in the name of Jesus. The pestilence has the trade mark of plague and disease as well.

These wicked powers may entangle your affairs and make you visionless. You won't be able to fulfill your dream because you are snared, captured and emptied. Hence, you become weak and powerless. A man in prison hardly controls his estate. All may vanish before he is released. The noisome pestilence devours everything because he was snared and imprisoned in the prison of life. A drunkard is imprisoned, drug addict is imprisoned, an adulterer is imprisoned, all he had may be auctioned or sold if he owe and couldn't pay. He may sell his property to meet urge for sex or drug. Such person needs deliverance. This is what this verse does.

The fowler is wicked. The devil and his agents represent fowler. They do things in utmost secrecy. They have their secret place as the Lord as well.

They strategize plans and position. They modify the snare to capture more soul to their kingdom and increase the number of captives. For this reason they change their traps and method. They are wickedly clever. The fowler will entice you until you fall prey and captured. I pray, you will not fall prey of the enemy in the name of Jesus.

Verse four says, *"He will cover you with His feathers and under His wings you will find refuge"* The feathers here means power of protection. It is a metaphor, referring to mother hen that gives protection to her chicks from danger. It means security, referring to God's power of protection. It means whoever comes to God is secured; whoever comes to him will not experience sudden death. It also mean, whatever you go in with, is secured. If you go under the feather of God with your money it is secured; robbers, thieves, burglars will not have access to it, because you are under the feather of God. If you are pregnant, you will deliver your baby without stress. If you are a student and you are under the feather of God, you will pass in flying color.

If you are under spiritual feather of God, no spiritual river shall sweep you away; no flood of darkness shall flood you away; no flood of darkness shall flood you away, no ocean of darkness shall swallow you. The feather of the Most High cannot be consumed by fire or pulled. The feather of God is supernatural. It is a feather cannot be contented with. The feather is supernaturally built. It is a feather nobody ever has, it is a unique feather indeed.

The Psalmist further says, ***"Under his wings you will find refuge"***. When the wing of God moves, it won't take you to a bad destination. It means, it shall take you to a place of safety, a place of peace and a place of favor. The wing of God will take you to mountain top. Heaven shall be your limit. When there is danger the wing of God will make you escape. No catapult or gunshot can bring you down, because you are covered in God's wings. The wing will make you a semi supernatural being, because the wing is supernatural. This is what the wing of God entails.

"Under his wings shalt thou trust" You trust his wings because God is powerful and in control. If God is not in control, you won't build the trust. Trust means you rely on it and it works. Trust means you don't doubt, trust means you don't entertain fear, trust means it is not counterfeit, trust means it is perfect and in order. You know there is no power that can contend with it, this is trust. I pray, the trust we have in God shall not be shaken by fear, it shall not be shaken by the threat of enemy, and shall not be shaken by arrow of darkness or evil gang up, in the name of Jesus. These can shake trust one has for wings of God. Lack of trust will make you shiver, affect your harvest and bring about downward financial slope in business while equilibrium position turns negative.

The Psalmist says, ***"His truth shall be thy shield and buckler"*** God is truthful, while the shield covers you; the buckler is what you wear around you in the spirit. The shield is to give you cover against evil arrow, evil bullet and evil stone. The shield of God is gun proof, arrow proof, stone proof, fire proof, flood proof and spiritual proof against any weapon. I pray that the shield of God shall cover you, in the name of Jesus.

There is grace of God in us, our spiritual life is protected by Divine Grace from the temptations of Satan, which are the snares of the fowler, and from the contagion of sin, which is a noisome pestilence. Great security is promised to believers in the midst of danger.

PRAYER POINTS

1. O Lord, deliver me from the snare of the fowler, in the name of Jesus.

2. Every noisome pestilence after my destiny, expire, in the name of Jesus.

3. Superlative feathers of God; cover me against evil attack, in the name of Jesus.

4. O Lord, let me swim in your palace of deliverance, in the name of Jesus.

5. Satanic bird catcher assign to turn me to bird in the spirit and captivate me, expire, in the name of Jesus.

6. Every bait assigned to lure me to sin, catch fire and roast to ashes, in the name of Jesus.

7. Every bait assign to lure me to failure, expire, in the name of Jesus.

8. Every bait assign to lure me to adultery and or fornication, expire, in the name of Jesus.

9. Every spiritual prison waiting my arrival, catch fire and roast to ashes, in the name of Jesus.

10. Every spiritual prison that harbors me be pulled down, in the name of Jesus.

11. Spirit of stealing, quit my life, in the name of Jesus.

12. Spirit of drunkenness, quit my life, in the name of Jesus.

13. Spirit of alcoholism, quit my life, in the name of Jesus.

14. Every noisome pestilence assign against me, expire, in the name of Jesus.

15. Powers assign to empty my wealth, expire, in the name of Jesus.

16. My destiny shall not cripple, in the name of Jesus.

17. Power of darkness shall not drain my purse in the name of Jesus.

18. Every dark locust assign against my harvest, expire, in the name of Jesus.

19. Any dark power assign to scatter my destiny, paralyze in the name of Jesus.

20. I shall fulfill my dream, in the name of Jesus.

21. Any devourer assign to devour my career, expire in the name of Jesus.

22. Every power assigned to render me weak and powerless, expire in the name of Jesus.

23. I shall not live in captivity, in the name of Jesus.

24. Every trap of darkness assign for me, catch your owner, in the name of Jesus.

25. Every chain of darkness design for me, break to pieces, in the name of Jesus.

26. Every plague from pit of hell, expire in the name of Jesus.

27. Every hopeless situation around me, expire in the name of Jesus.

28. Power assign to destroy my family with hunger, we are not your candidate, expire, in the name of Jesus.

29. Spirit of debt assigned to swallow my finance, expire in the name of Jesus.

30. I shall not borrow to feed, in the name of Jesus.

31. Every arrow of nakedness fired against me backfire in the name of Jesus.

32. I shall not dwell in the valley, in the name of Jesus.

33. I shall not be naked in the name of Jesus.

34. My destiny shall not sink, in the name of Jesus.

35. Divine protection; locate me, in the name of Jesus.

36. Suicide spirit monitoring my home, expire, in the name of Jesus.

37. I am delivered from bondage of darkness in the name of Jesus.

38. I shall enjoy maximum security in the Lord in the name of Jesus.

39. O Heaven, lift me to the destined position God made for me, in the name of Jesus.

40. O Lord, carry me in your wing in the name of Jesus.

41. I trust in the Lord, I abide in his name, in the name of Jesus.

42. Every doubt in my spirit that will make me lose helpers disappear; in the name of Jesus.
43. I recover my shield seized in the spirit, in the name of Jesus.

CHAPTER 3

THOU SHALL NOT BE AFRAID

"Thou shalt not be afraid for the terror by night; nor for the arrow that flieth by day; 6. Nor for the pestilence that walketh in darkness; nor for the destruction that wasteth at noonday" Psalm 91:5-6

Verse 5 gives us convenience; we have shield and buckler that protects us from the enemy. Now this verse encourages us of thou shall not be afraid, don't entertain fear, the shield of God is with you, the buckler is there for you as well. Don't be afraid of terror by night, which means terror move and operate by night. Terror carry out wickedness at night, terror kills at night, terror destroy at night, terror kidnap at night, terror wage war at night, terror rob at night. These, you must not be fear. God says, "Leave everything to me". What should you do? The answer is, pray to God and declare; "Terror I declare you null and void in my sleep.

All terror that come in my sleep, I command you to paralyze. All terror that come to consume my house, when I am asleep, I speak against you, in the name of Jesus. All terror that come to rob me at night, I command you to go blind and paralyze". These are what you declare at night before bed time

Be confident, don't have shallow belief. Do not be afraid because you have a living God, the man of war. When you have man of war, and any power declare war against you in the night, who will fail? It is the power that comes to fight God, because God is with you. Though you slept alone, you are not alone, God is with you. Whoever is with God, is majority. Don't say they come in multitude, they will overcome you; it is a lie. Don't be afraid.

It is written, ***"nor by the arrow that fly by day"***. This tells us, arrow fly by day. When enemy shoot arrow, they shoot arrow by day. During the day they see the person they want to fire. It is during the day, they aim at the person. At night you may shoot indiscriminately, but during the day you shoot arrow because you can aim your enemy. When you fire arrow it moves fast and is poisonous. Those that fire arrow by day mean business, they want to kill. Those that fire arrow by day, are strategic, they aim the enemy and get them down. They aim their target well, they are snipers.

Arrow is not something you play with. We have different types of arrow. It can be arrow of untimely death. It can be arrow of stagnancy, arrow of failure, arrow of bareness, arrow of emptiness etc. These arrows fly by day and are shot during the day. The pouch where arrows are kept is a house of death, house of confusion, house of negatives of life. Anybody that fire arrow is demonic; all he thinks and does is evil. That power must be rebuked.

Verse 6 says, *"nor for the pestilence that walks in darkness"*. Such pestilence is not ordinary pestilence; it loves darkness and is wicked. It is at night snake crawls around, it is at night evil spirit walks freely, and furious at night. When men slept, they cause havoc and confusion; they are dangerous in the environment and sow evil seed in the garden of life. Armed robber perfects their acts at night. They do it quietly and leave quietly.

"Nor by destruction that wasteth at noon day". So many destructions happen during the day. Destruction happens in office where pen is used to defraud company, state or nation. They cause havoc to the destiny of people. They waste lives and destroy destiny. They amputate the future of many; they don't want people to grow. They may hold meeting at night, but they carry out destruction in the day. Power that destroys shall not locate us, in the name of Jesus. Amen. Pestilence that destroys can be human or satanic, it

can be spiritual or physical as well. Pestilence is used as metaphor, it is known as pest that destroys. Pestilence is anything that destroy, that devalue or bring one down.

The Psalmist says, ***"You shall not be afraid"*** This is a statement of confidence and authority. The reason is the Lord provides shelter and refuge for you. You have good foundation that gives comfort and peace. A man or woman under the shadow of God has nothing to fear. No dark power, witches or wizard, occult or strange darkness can overcome you. All you need is, to summon courage and face the enemy.

Fear exposes one to danger. Fear causes wound in the heart. Fear gives birth in multiple if not checked quickly. You must uproot plantation of fear in your heart. The heart beats when fear occupies it. But the Lord says, fear not; you should not be afraid of terror by night, nor the arrow that flies by day because He is with you. This means arrow of darkness flies by day. Such arrow will not locate you because you are under the protection of God. The Lord provides you with protective garment.

This means every arrow fired against you shall not locate you or consume you. The arrows are dead on arrival. Shooters of such arrows shall be frustrated and count losses. They won't have power over you or gain advantage over you. Any arrow fired against you shall not stand. No arrow of darkness shall pull you down or kill you.

There are different types of arrow. Arrows are named after what they do. We have arrow of untimely death that causes sudden death. There is arrow of poverty, fired to make victim poor and financially stagnant. We have arrow of hatred, which leads to hatred without reason. We have arrow of stagnancy and backwardness, arrow of delay, arrow of failure etc. Arrows are bad, arrows are killers of destiny, arrow demotes; it devalues life and causes agony and sadness. This is what the Psalmist saw before he said "Do not be afraid, I have fought the battle before it started. You have won the battle before it ever started. You are a hero and a conqueror".

The Psalmist says; "Do not fear the terror of the night". He knows terror looms at night. There are spiritual and physical terrors at night. In the spirit, enemies come to oppress in the sleep. They feed you with demonic foods so that you count losses or die sudden death. Some molest you with sex in the dream to cause infertility, poverty, joblessness, fear, sickness and disease. All these, devalue life. There are fearful dreams enemy use to terrify people, like, being pursued by masquerade in the dream, road-block and barriers in the dream, slavery in the dream, being robbed in the dream etc. The Lord says, don't fear, terror of the night is not your portion.

Physical terror in the night abound. Many souls are demonically summoned at night at T junction, evil forest; evil river, evil altar and evil homes. They do incantation at night naked or half naked. They invoke evil to names, marriages, children, family, works and offices. They are merciless; and happy whenever they carry out such ignoble act. Plagues happen at night as well and it's confirmed it happens during the day. The first born of Egypt fell to the sword of death at night. Powers of darkness carry out evil at night undisturbed. Kidnappers and assassins find it comfortable and unchallenged at night. They lure people to terror at night. Verily, verily, I say unto you, the Lord, Yahweh says, thou shall not fear the terror of night. He is always there for you.

Night times are horrible. Pestilence stalks in it, meaning pestilence find it easy to operate in darkness. Darkness is a time for demonic operation. Every evil enemy carry out in the dark are seen by God as if it is day time. David says in the book of Psalm, ***"Even the darkness will not be dark to you; the night will shine like the day, for darkness is as light to you" Psalm 139:12.*** No wonder our God says, "do not be afraid, I see them even in darkness" Hallelujah.

The Psalmist is conscious of time, he mentioned day, night, and noonday. Whenever and wherever it comes, God is able to defend you. The assaults of enemies will not consume you, in the name of Jesus. Amen. The fact is, in the midst of great darkness living without His truth and freedom is like wallowing in the pit. No hope or freedom can be found there. The truth is, this world is in darkness, since sin first entered the earth at the hiss of the enemy's lies.

A plague is an illness that people catch from each other if one person becomes ill, many other people that live near become ill as well. There is assurance of protection and love for us. Even if we become ill through plague, God will protect us after we die. We will live with him in heaven, his home. And God will continue to protect us from evil spirit.

PRAYER POINTS

1. Spirit of fear quit my life, in the name of Jesus.
2. Every plantation of confusion in the garden of my life, dry up, in the name of Jesus.
3. O Lord, decorate me with shield of victory in the name of Jesus.
4. Every terror by night against me, expire in the name of Jesus.
5. Every warfare against me, scatter in the name of Jesus.
6. Every wickedness of the wicked against my soul, expire, in the name of Jesus.
7. Every terror against me, I declare you null and void, in the name of Jesus.
8. O Lord, give me confidence to excel in my career, in the name of Jesus.

9. O Lord, turn me to man of war that win battles, in the name of Jesus.

10. Every warfare against me scatter, in the name of Jesus.

11. Every terror that come to attack me in my sleep, paralyze in the name of Jesus.

12. I fire arrow of God, to scatter the camp of the enemy, in the name of Jesus.

13. Every arrow of untimely death fired against me, backfire, in the name of Jesus.

14. Every arrow of stagnancy fired against me, backfire, in the name of Jesus.

15. Every arrow of failure fired against me, backfire, in the name of Jesus.

16. Every arrow of bareness fired against me, backfire, in the name of Jesus.

17. Every arrow of emptiness fired against me, backfire, in the name of Jesus.

18. Power assign to empty my house, you are a liar, expire, in the name of Jesus.

19. Every pestilence that walks in darkness to destroy my destiny your time is up, expire, in the name of Jesus.

20. Power assign to attack me in my sleep shall fail, in the name of Jesus.

21. Every seed of darkness planted in the garden of my life, wither and die, in the name of Jesus.

22. Satanic weed growing in the garden of my life, wither in the name of Jesus.

23. Every power assign to waste me be wasted in the name of Jesus.

24. Power assigned to amputate my future, expire, in the name of Jesus.

25. Every dark meeting held to destroy me, scatter in the name of Jesus.

26. O Lord, give me authority over my enemy, in the name of Jesus.

27. O Lord, provide shelter of peace and breakthrough for me, in the name of Jesus.

28. Witches and wizards assign to give me command in the spirit in order to reap failure, expire, in the name of Jesus.

29. Stranger of darkness disappear in my life, in the name of Jesus.

30. Every fear that exposed me to danger, expire, in the name of Jesus.

31. Lord Jesus, heal the wound in my heart, in the name of Jesus.

32. Every arrow that flies by day against me, backfire to your sender, in the name of Jesus.

33. O Lord, provide me arrow proof protective garment, in the name of Jesus.

34. Powers that oppress me in my sleep; expire, in the name of Jesus.

35. Evil caterers assign to feed me in my sleep, paralyze in your kitchen, in the name of Jesus.

36. Dream of failure in my life; expire, in the name of Jesus.

37. Dream of bareness in my sleep; expire, in the name of Jesus.

38. Every road-block of darkness fashioned against me, scatter in the name of Jesus.

39. Every attack of sickness and diseases as a result of night attack, expire in the name of Jesus.

40. Evil summon of my soul, backfire in the name of Jesus.

41. Every ritual carried out to attack me, backfire in the name of Jesus.

42. Plague of darkness against me, scatter, in the name of Jesus.

43. Robbers of soul, expire in the name of Jesus.

44. O Lord, defend me by your power, in the name of Jesus.

CHAPTER 4

A PRAYER OF PROMISE AND HOPE

"A thousand shall fall at thy side, and ten thousand at thy right hand; but it shall not come near thee. Only with thine eyes shalt thou behold and see the reward of the wicked" Psalm 91:7-8

This chapter, verses 7-8 shall be treated at its face value (physical) and spiritual (spirit). We always take it as enemies' death by our sides in a thousand and in ten thousands and merely seeing it by our eyes. Yes, there is nothing God cannot do. He can protect you and kill thousands that wage war against you. The battle may not be physical, but in metaphor.

A thousand tells you, big danger may come, ten thousand at the right hand; it raises from a thousand to ten thousand. It means, danger may increase, but it will not near you. The danger may be one, it will not come near you, the danger may be ten it will not come near you. This means, you are free from every small and big danger. When people says, "The flood sweep people away"; it means it won't be your portion, because the Lord shall protect you. If it is said; accident consumes people, you will not be a partaker. This is what a thousand, and or, ten thousand represents. You will only see it by your eyes, or hear of it. It shall not come near you. Why? Because there is buckler around you, there is shield around you; as you are in the presence of God, where nothing can harm you.

The Lord counts you righteous. The righteous don't fall victim anyhow. The righteous is always protected by God. The righteous don't count losses. The righteous cannot be mocked. The righteous are powerful. I pray, you shall be counted righteous today, in the name of Jesus.

There is promise of, with your eyes you will see it, but shall not come near you, but the wicked shall be consumed. This is their reward. Their reward is untimely death. Their reward is failure. Their reward is suicide. Their reward is agony. Their reward is sorrow. Their reward is cry. The reward of the wicked shall be for the wicked, in Jesus name.

Israel was a great nation in the past. During the time of David, he conquered many nations around it and made Jerusalem the capital. Bitter hatred and coalition of enemy against David was futile. The enemies of Israel bowed because God was with David. ***"David grew stronger and stronger, while the house of Saul grew weaker and weaker" 2 Samuel 3:1b***. Later in life, David conquered other nations around him and made them vassal states.

Hear what the Lord says of David. ***"Now therefore so shalt thou say unto my servant David, Thus saith the LORD of hosts, I took thee from the sheepcote, from following the sheep, to be ruler over my people, over Israel: And I was with thee*** *whithersoever thou wentest, and have cut off all thine enemies out of thy sight, and have made thee a great name, like unto the name of the great men that are in the earth. Moreover I will appoint a place for my people Israel, and will plant them, that they may dwell in a place of their own, and move no more; neither shall the children of wickedness afflict them anymore, as beforetime. And as since the time that I commanded judges to be over my people Israel, and have caused thee to rest from all thine enemies. Also the LORD telleth thee that he will make thee an house"* 2 *Samuel 7:8-11*

We can see that God was with David, he subdued his enemies in thousands (Saul lineage- the Benjamite) and later put all enemies around him under his feet in ten thousands! This is physical aspect of it.

The spiritual aspect can be likened to the pestilence and plague mentioned in verse 6 of previous chapter. Pestilence and plague are agents of great devastation when it comes. Devastation and calamity may happen but it shall not come near thee. There was plague of Ebola it did not touch you, there was also plague of corona virus you were not consumed. This is God's protection for your life. Thousands of people died, God preserved you. It is God's doing. The plague that killed the firstborn in Egypt near the dwelling of the Israelites, it entered not into them. This is spiritual battle against the Egyptians that brought physical testimonies to the children of Israel.

In *2 Samuel 24:15, "So the Lord sent a plague on Israel from the morning until the end of the time designated, and seventy thousands of the people from Dan to Beersheba died"*. Spirituality comes to play here when the Angel of death wanted to stretch his hand to Jerusalem. The Lord commanded him, and said *"Enough! Withdraw your hand"* David was spared. Though he was the one that sinned, God showed him favour and mercy. The children of Israel that died are not David's enemy but "scapegoats". God shows, ten thousand may die at his command and spare his beloved. If God can do this to Israel what is more to your enemy.

PRAYER POINTS

1. O Lord, equip me with weapons of war to defeat my enemy, in the name of Jesus.

2. Any power that rise against me, meet double failure, in the name of Jesus.

3. O Lord, let there be confusion in the camp of my enemy in the name of Jesus.

4. O Lord, throw your bomb in the midst of enemies that gather against me, in the name of Jesus.

5. Workers of iniquity against my life, paralyze in the name of Jesus.

6. Every danger that surrounds me, scatter in the name of Jesus.

7. O Lord, pull down the pillars enemy rely on, in the name of Jesus.

8. A thousand may come against me, they shall fail, in the name of Jesus.

9. With my eyes shall I see the fall of enemies that rise up against me, in the name of Jesus.

10. Trouble shooters around me fall by my side and rise no more in the name of Jesus.

11. Every battle against me, scatter in the name of Jesus.

12. Every weapon fashioned against me shall not prosper, in the name of Jesus.

13. My destiny shall not be wasted in the hands of enemy, in the name of Jesus.

14. O Lord, make me great in the midst of my enemy, in the name of Jesus.

15. O Lord, make me a conqueror, not a failure, in the name of Jesus.

16. O Lord, make my house, a house of joy and peace, in the name of Jesus.

17. Every gathering against me, scatter in the name of Jesus.

18. O Lord, let me grow stronger and stronger before my enemy, in the name of Jesus.

19. O Lord, let my enemy grow weaker and weaker, in the name of Jesus.

20. O Lord, silence powers assign to bring down my lineage, in the name of Jesus.

21. O Lord put my enemy under my feet, in the name of Jesus.

22. My star, arise and shine, in the name of Jesus.

23. Calamity shall not come close to my house, in the name of Jesus.

24. Enough is enough sudden death shall not visit my house in the name of Jesus.

25. Enough is enough, famine shall not have place in my family, in the name of Jesus.

26. Violent angels of heaven, arise in your anger, destroy dark powers around me, in the name of Jesus.

27. Every evil eye monitoring me, go blind in the name of Jesus.

28. Blood of Jesus, arise, scatter works of darkness in my environment in the name of Jesus.

29. Flying witchcraft around me, crash land, in the name of Jesus.

30. O Lord, establish my name in heaven, in the name of Jesus.

31. By fire, by thunder, I war in the spirit against my enemies in the name of Jesus.

32. Every door that closed against me as a result of enemy's attack open in the name of Jesus.

33. O Lord, let your agenda for my life stand, in the name of Jesus.

34. Every witchcraft prayer targeted against my destiny, backfire in the name of Jesus.

35. I shall live long and not die, in the name of Jesus.

36. My ladder of glory, appear, in the name of Jesus.

37. Windows of heaven, open and bless me, in the name of Jesus.

38. Enemy shall not abort my glory, in the name of Jesus.

39. O Lord, satisfy me with long life, in the name of Jesus.

40. Rain of abundant mercy, be my portion, in the name of Jesus.

41. O Lord, reveal secrets of my enemy to me, in the name of Jesus.

42. I thank you Lord, for your mercy upon me, in the name of Jesus.

43. I thank God, he renew my strength.

CHAPTER 5

O LORD PROTECT ME

"Because thou hast made the LORD, which is my refuge, even the most High, thy habitation; there shall be no evil befall thee, neither shall any plague come nigh thy dwelling. For he shall give his angels charge over thee, to keep thee in all thy ways. They shall bear thee up in their hands, lest thou dash thy foot against a stone" Psalm 91:9-12

Here comes the power of angel. All we say earlier in the previous chapter mean angels dwell around God's habitation. Angel that stops spirit of death is there. Angel is a spirit. There is no how you will enter the habitation of God without being seen by angel of God. The angels will overpower and stop contrary power to carry out evil. Angel will kill if God commands it to kill. Angels are agent of the Lord Almighty Father. They listen to no one, than

God. If God tells angel to carry out a mission he won't turn back until it is carried out.

When Angel Michael was sent to Daniel and was stopped by the Persian he did not turn back, he was there for twenty one days, until he delivered answer to Daniel. When angel is sent by God, and say "Go and deliver" he will make sure he delivers. When angel went to Elizabeth the wife of Zechariah he delivered his message; so were messages to Zechariah and Mary, the mother of Jesus. There is no power that can stop or terrorize an angel on the way. This is the reason God uses angel. Angels increase faith of people under the shadow of God. As you are under the shadow of God, angel of God shall guide you. Angel takes your request to Almighty Father.

Angels are in charge 24/7 to protect you. They won't allow you to strike your leg on anything dangerous. The stone here connotes stumbling block, the stone is not ordinary, it can be a river or sea, a mountain or valley. The angel will guide you against danger of any kind. It is talking about what can bring downfall. The angel will guide you against such. God will destroy every stone of poverty assign to bring poverty to your life in the name of Jesus. Stone of death will not have power over you. Stone of debt will not consume your finance. Angels will guide your foot against stone of calamity. Stone of mockery will not have power over you. Stone of nakedness will not have power over you. All manner of negative stones shall not be your portion, in the name of Jesus.

This stone is not ordinary stone. It is talking about hard problem. When you say, you have stone like problem or ironic problem, it is a problem that is very difficult to surmount. With such problem you won't know how to go about it. The Lord says, the angel will not allow your leg to strike it. This means you will be guided seriously against it. It means you will see it but shall not come near you.

It means calamity is around but you won't go close to it. Instead of you to take the path to it, angel of God will guide you to take another path because he guides your feet against it.

The writer knows the value of refuge. He did not say, our refuge, he personalizes it. He was a righteous man and sold the idea to others. He tried to convince us that righteousness is good, and that one should do what he did, to take refuge under the shadow of God and enjoy protection of God. He takes refuge in the habitation of God to possess his possession. When you are in your habitation, you have shelter over your head. Your habitation means, you are not a beggar. Your habitation means, you are not afraid. Your habitation means, you have peace of mind because the habitation is of the Lord no one can question.

The Psalmist says, no evil shall come near you. In God's habitation evil cannot come near you because God is there. Look at Aso Rock where

Head of State lives, or White House in America, you can't wake in the morning and go there, you will be questioned, if you don't have genuine reason to be there you can be detained or jailed. Think of God's habitation the Almighty, if you are in this habitation, no one can molest you. No one can threaten or send message of fear or terror to you. Who is the messenger that will deliver the message? Before he moves close to God's habitation, the leg will paralyze, he will go blind, confuse and useless. As you are in God's habitation today, any power assign to attack you shall paralyze, in the name of Jesus. Mention the name of the evil intended against you; it shall not come near you. This is confirmation that there is power that pass power. This is confirmation that there is power that overrides other powers. And what is the power? It is power of God.

To make God your dwelling is always a good choice. No power can subdue God. You are a potential winner once you make him your habitation. The habitation of God is unique. It is a place you never regret to know, visit or occupy. You visit such place in trance or in the dream. You see the picture and fall in love. You abide in it because of its safety, shelter, and uniqueness of peace.

No harm befalls people that make God his place of habitation. No arrow fired at you gets at you. You won't experience fire outbreak in his habitation. No one steals there. No robber operates there. No kidnap or rituals take place there. The ritual there is praises to the Almighty, with siren of love, peace and joy. Base on this, ***Psalm 91:10 says, "There shall no evil befall thee, neither shall any plague come near thy dwelling"***. You don't record casualty in God's habitation, no harm can befall you; no disaster will come near your tent. It is a promise to the letter of those who makes God their habitation. Because they are righteous, they will flourish like palm tree.

Habitation of God is full of angels carrying out one duty or the other to ensure peace, love, oneness and joy. Everything done connotes perfection. You won't or count loss in God's habitation. The angels are with trumpets of victory every day. This was revealed to John the Beloved in the book of ***Revelation 8:2. "And I saw the seven angels who stand before God, and to them were given seven trumpets".*** Seven angels with seven trumpets mean much. Do you know the meaning of seven (7) in the spirit? Seven means, perfection, complete, all, rest, finished, satisfaction. You shall be satisfied in the Lord's habitation with perfection, in all things and you will say, "It is finished" in the word of Jesus on the cross.

God's habitation connotes victory and breakthrough. His habitation is gold, street is gold, environment gold, altar is gold. The angels have golden heart with golden service to the Lord. *"Another angel, who had a golden censer, come and stood at the altar. He was given much incense to offer, with the prayers of all the saints, on the golden altar before the throne" Revelation 8:3.* God gives golden opportunity. It will be a tragedy to lose or miss heaven.

The habitation of God is where you enjoy river of life, water of life and ocean of life. Thirst will never be your portion. You are daily satisfied with water of life. *"Then the angel showed me the river of the water of life, as clear as crystal, flowing from the throne of God and of the Lamb" Revelation 22:1.* Water of life symbolize peace, end of thirst or thirst free life, joy, good harvest, fruitfulness etc.

You count gains in the habitation of God. Satan is jealous and arrogant in this respect. He wants to control, sidelining God in heaven. God knows what entails in his habitation. When Satan rebel, he was casted to the earth. He lost his place in heaven. This makes him and the fallen angels' bitter, with mind to revenge on men and women on earth. The righteous runs to God in his habitation, in prayer where peace reigns. Satan knew how fancy heaven is; he fights tooth and nail to stop us, anytime he remembers how he was hurled down to earth. This is the remark. ***"And there was war in heaven. Michael and his angels fought against the dragon, and the dragon and his angels fought back. But he was not strong enough, and they lost their place in heaven. The great dragon was hurled down that ancient serpent called the devil, or Satan, who leads the whole world astray. He was hurled to the earth, and his angels with him"*** ***Revelation 12:7-9.***

Brethren, Satan is bitter any moment you think of God's habitation. He tested it and knew how good it was before who were created. Ever since then, he picks you and me as enemy. If you are not in his camp, he hates you. God is ready to "Command his angels of you", to protect and fight on your behalf. No power or personality can withstand God if he arises for your sake. When it was fire for fire in heaven Satan lost out. When God commands his angels of you, heaven will open and support you in whatever you do. When God command his angels of you, you shall win every battle in the dream. When God command his angels of you; fear, sorrow, agony, stagnation, backwardness shall flee.

The Lord is your support, the angels *"will lift you up in their hands, so that you will not strike your foot against a stone" Psalm 91:12.* Brethren, you are in save hands of God every time you abide in his habitation. The secret place of God shall not elude you, in the name of Jesus. Amen.

PRAYER POINTS

1. Angels of God; dwell in my habitation and let peace reign in my life, in the name of Jesus.

2. Angel of God; stretch your hand from God's habitation to my house for protection, in the name of Jesus.

3. Angel of God, rebuke spirit of death in my life in the name of Jesus.

4. Good news from heaven, locate me today, in the name of Jesus.

5. I am delivered from the wicked agenda of Satan, in the name of Jesus.

6. My faith shall not fail, in the name of Jesus.

7. Angel of God; protect me, in the name of Jesus.

8. Every stone of darkness assign in the spirit against my success, break to pieces, in the name of Jesus.

9. Every stone of darkness that causes untimely death, fashion against me, break, in the name of Jesus.

10. Every stone of darkness erected to cause sickness and diseases, break to pieces, in the name of Jesus.

11. I shall not strike my leg against stone of darkness in the name of Jesus.

12. Every dark river flowing into my life, dry up, in the name of Jesus.

13. Every stumbling block on my way, disappear in the name of Jesus.

14. O Lord, guide me against danger, in the name of Jesus.

15. Every hand of evil stretched to me by Satan, wither, in the name of Jesus.

16. Every stone of debt in my investment; expire, in the name of Jesus.

17. Every problem people says how can it be solved, O Lord turn it to stepping stone of breakthrough in the name of Jesus.

18. Calamity of disgrace assign to swallow my joy, expire, in the name of Jesus.

19. Spirit of righteousness come upon me, in the name of Jesus.

20. Enemy shall not take my possession from me, in the name of Jesus.

21. Beggarly spirit, quit my life, in the name of Jesus.

22. Situation that brings peace of mind be my portion, in the name of Jesus.

23. Any move to silence me by enemy, scatter in the name of Jesus.

24. I shall not make wrong choice in life, in the name of Jesus.

25. O Lord, give me spirit to praise you, in the name of Jesus.

26. I am like a palm tree with multiple blessings of God, in the name of Jesus.

27. O Lord, bow my trumpet of victory over enemies in the name of Jesus.

28. O Lord, perfect your deliverance in my life, in the name of Jesus.

29. I shall reap success and breakthrough in the habitation of God in the name of Jesus.

30. O Lord, give me golden heart in the name of Jesus.

31. O Lord, let your altar of prayer in my home be altar of God, in the name of Jesus.

32. O Lord, provide me with water of life that sustains one till eternity, in the name of Jesus.

33. Satan, I cast your work out of my house, in the name of Jesus.

34. Every fallen angel that resides in my house pack your load and leave, in the name of Jesus.

35. Every dark angel on assignment of revenge because of my prayer, be disgraced, in the name of Jesus.

36. Every dragon in the garden of my life, I break your head, in the name of Jesus.

37. Ancient serpent attacking me in my sleep, expire, in the name of Jesus.

38. I shall not be led astray, in the journey of life, in the name of Jesus.

39. Every bitterness in my life, expire, in the name of Jesus.

40. O Lord, command your angel to protect me, in the name of Jesus.

41. O Lord, give me support to climb ladder of breakthrough, in the name of Jesus.

42. Oh heaven, open and favor me, in the name of Jesus.

43. Spirit of agony, flee my life, in the name of Jesus.

44. I thank you Lord, for your love for me, in the name of Jesus.

CHAPTER 6

O LORD EMPOWER ME

"Thou shalt tread upon the lion and adder: the young lion and the dragon shalt thou trample under feet. Because he hath set his love upon me, therefore I will deliver him: I will set him on high, because he hath known my name." Psalm 91:13-14

The foundation these two verses rest on is the acknowledgement of God's name. Acknowledgement of God's name means, to respect and recognize God and Jesus as the Lord and Savior. Acknowledgment of God's name means submission to his Holy Name. Knowing God's name means to know what he can and will do. Knowing God is to focus on Him as a deliverer of souls from Egypt and taking us to our Promised Land. Knowing God's name is to establish the rational phenomenon of history, "God of Abraham, God of Isaac and God of Jacob" We acknowledged what he did with the Patriarch. We acknowledge his name to give wisdom and surmount problems; also, to enjoy the infinite grace and goodness of him. We acknowledge God of his power and might over all creatures.

The power he passed to us to tread upon the lion and the cobra; is the same power passed to us that make us trample the great lion and the serpent. There are wild animals of repute to kill and destroy. They are wild animal feared by men and women. Serpent was the first creature that brought Adam and Eve down. It has been a long time enemy of mankind. The bible says, you can trample upon it, meaning, you shall subdue your enemy and put them in permanent disgrace.

The Psalmist says, you will tread upon lion, when you tread upon lion, it means God gives you special power. The power you can't define or explain. The power is awesome. Before you can fight and trample upon lion, it means you fight and win stubborn situation. Lion is the most fearful animal in the jungle. If you tread upon it and win, you feel elated. When you think of what happen in the past, you will give glory to the ALMIGHTY. When you count your blessings, you know it is miraculous.

The only person that tread upon lion was Daniel, God was with him. The lion did not consume him, while those who were thrown into the den of lion were consumed. The lion break their bones and ate them all. This is the animal God says you will tread upon. Because of you, God shall paralyze their power and make them empty. It means they shall be toothless bulldog. It means God shall cage their heart. God removed shall remove heart of wickedness in them. All their claws are removed spiritually. Their teeth are removed spiritually. Even their fearful appearance is removed from your heart so that you won't have fear. These are the condition that can make you tread upon lion and be fearless. Ordinarily, if you see a dead lion you will run. But now, the Psalmist says you shall tread upon it. You can see how God manifests his power. What you believe is impossible, God says is possible. The door you believe cannot open, God says, it shall open. The position you think you can't occupy, God says you shall occupy and rule. What you think you can't do in life. God says you can do. You say, "This project will consume my finance and empty me", God says you will do it and make profit. That expense is lion and you shall overcome it, in the name of Jesus.

The lion, the adder and the dragon are dangerous animals. What the Psalmist tells is, no matter the problem in your life, God will see you through. The Psalmist compares it to lion, young lion, adder, and dragon. There are strong problems that need to be addressed in life. Any strong problem that comes your way, God shall solve it. When lion roars everybody around keeps quiet, every animal will run. But in your own case if everybody runs you will stand like David and kill the Goliath.

The cobra and lion represents fierce enemies to humanity that can be subdued if we know the importance and the names of God. These animals are mentioned to represent dark powers that attack destiny of people. They turn victims to mincemeat and attack their dream life. They are captains of tragedy. Their look is terrible, fearful, fierce and full of wickedness. They don't dwell in secret place of the Most High. They are alien in God's presence.

The two verses 12-13, gives assurance and boldness to face, it conquer and destroy works of darkness, because the Lord loves you. This is possible because the Lord handle every situation with perfection. The reason, he has many names tell His character and value. We shall look at a number of his names and unique role they play later in this chapter.

Verse 14 says, ***"Because he hath set his love upon me, therefore will I deliver him; I will set him on high, because he hath known my name".*** The name of the Lord saves, when danger comes and you shout, "Jesus!" You will see that something special will happen. You will have confidence because you believe in the name. "Because he hath set his love upon me" means, you must love God. Love is very important. When you love God, God will love you. When you love God, he will open the door you think won't open to you. Before you can say you love God, you must be far from sin. To love God means you are prayerful. Before you can say you love God, it means you love your neighbor. If you love God, don't lay hands on what is evil. If you love God, he will deliver you of evil that comes your way. This is the power of the Almighty. The simple rule is, "If you do good, I do good to you, if you do bad, I leave you".

"I will set him on high", means, he will move you from the valley to mountain top. It means, he will take you from state of poverty to riches. He will move you from state of stagnancy to better height. He will move you from failure to profit. It is a power that reverses evil to good and bad to good. This is the power of God when he delivers you. He said, he will set you high because you know his name. The road is clear for you when you know His name and use it well. Here you can mention many names of God like; El-shadai, Elohi, Elyon, Yahweh etc. There are names of God you should know how to use. They shall be treated in this chapter. The name is with meaning and should be applied rightly. You apply right prayer to right situation, so when you need wealth, call the name of God that relates to it. When you need safety call the name of God that relate to it. When you need fruitfulness, use the right name, God will know you are very close to him that is why you know him by Name. God in his throne will be happy. He will move on his throne and say, "My son knows me, my daughter knows me, by my name". For this, he will answer you and deliver you because you know him by name.

1. God is Elohim- He is your Creator

"In the beginning God created the heavens and the earth" Genesis 1:1. God creates the universe with divine creative imagination. God who created you in his own image wouldn't leave you behind. You are the apple of God's eye. He won't leave you in the hand of the enemy, if you count on his name.

2. God is Elohm Chayim- He is the Living God

Our God is a living God, he can't die; He is an everlasting God. Jesus that came in human form was crucified, he died, was buried and he resurrected the third day. Joshua said, *"Today you will know that the living God is among you"*. *Joshua 3:10*. Our living God will rescue you and protect you. It is only Christians that can boast of a living God in Christ. All founder of other religion are dead, and buried. They are in there grave. Images are worthless, so are other gods.

3. God is Abba- He is your Father

God is our Father; we are not slaves to him. He treats us as children, the reason He accepts us in his secret place. If you identify yourself with God, he identifies himself with you. You can't be a push over in the presence of God. This is what the Bible says:

"For you did not receive a spirit that makes you a slave again to fear, but you received the spirit of Sonship. And by him we cry, Abba, Father" Romans 8:15

4. God is Jehovah-Jireh-The Lord will provide

At every point we lost hope, God provides us with peace and expectation, if we are in his presence. It is when you are in his presence, he sees you. If you are with Satan, he turns his back at you, as if he doesn't see you. Abraham was with God when he directed Isaac his only son should be sacrificed to him. At the point Abraham took knife to sacrifice Isaac, the Angel of the Lord called unto him from heaven---Don't lay a hand on the boy. At this point, God provided ram for sacrifice. The place was named Jehovah-Jireh by Abraham.

5. God is Jehovah-Shallom- The Lord is peace

God is the only One able to give us peace in his secret place. His peace passes all understanding. God will show up strong on your behalf and bring deliverance to you. The fear that filled your heart will receive healing of peace. No matter the source of darkness, it shall disappear and expire. Even in time of struggles, God will appear in your situation. This is Jehovah- Shallom for you. The peace of God shall reign in your life. Amen.

6. God is Jehovah Rapha-God the Healer

This name brings comfort and hope to those who pray for healing. In the presence of God, sickness and disease related problems have solution before God-Jehovah Rapha. The Lord in his fortress stretch hand of deliverance upon his people. They are healed and delivered of illness, sickness and disease, brokenness and painful circumstances. If you raise your hands to God and pray, you shall receive answer according to your faith.

7. God is Yahweh Nissi-The Lord is my Banner

Our basic need from God is protection. This is the reason the Psalmist calls Him "My refuge" The Lord gives and provides us protection, leadership and deliverance. The children of Israel wre protected from multiple enemies. They crushed their enemies without stress, unless they void the Ten Commandments.

8. God is Yahweh Yireh - The Lord Will Provide

Our God is there to provide our needs. He knows better when to provide for us. He doesn't dance to our call because he knows tomorrow, we don't know. He is faithful, He is able, and nothing is too difficult for Him. He does things when it should be. Sometimes His timing is different to ours, He did not forget us, He is there for us and will definitely provide for us.

9. God is El Shaddai- He is God Almighty

The God of heaven and earth is all powerful. He is the Mighty one. He is the One we run to for protection and provision of our needs. In his secret place are our needs in protection and good care. He is our source of comfort. No battle can consume you because the Almighty is there for you. Don't trust human strength but God.

10.God is El Roi- The God who sees

God sees everywhere, every time, every day. Since He sees everywhere, he stretches hand of hope and deliverance to us. He is our guard. He sees us when we feel lonely. He sees us when trouble is around the corner. He saw to the plight of Hagar, He saw to loneliness of Elijah and saved the situation.

11.God is El Elyon- God Most High

The name connotes God is above all gods. He is the Lord Most High, He reigns supreme. He is greater than forces of darkness, witches and wizards, idols and evil altar. He is in control, he never lose battle. He will never lose His power and might. This is one of his character- El-Elyon. He is Mighty, He is Lord. He is exalted over all. In his secret place emanates strength and might.

12.God is Yahweh-The Lord

This name is delivered from the Hebrew word "I AM". The Lord exists and is there for us. He showed his might when he liberated the Israelites from bondage in Egypt. When he appeared to

Moses and instructed him to go to Egypt and liberate Israel, he revealed his name to him. He said, tell Pharaoh, "I AM" sent you. The Lord is "I AM who I AM". Fear not, I AM is with you, even in tribulation and in time of chaos.

PRAYER POINTS

1. O Lord, I thank you for me to know you as my personal Lord and Savior.

2. I thank my God, who will not let me languish in captivity.

3. I thank my God, who enables me dwell in safety, in the name of Jesus.

4. The plans of enemy against me shall not stand, in the name of Jesus.

5. O Lord, give me power to trample upon serpent and scorpion in the name of Jesus.

6. Every dark lion assign against me in the spirit, expire, in the name of Jesus.

7. Destructive animals in the garden of my life, expire, in the name of Jesus.

8. Destructive animals in the garden of my life, expire, in the name of Jesus.

9. Serpent shall not tempt or destroy my calling or career in the name of Jesus.

10. O Lord, let my enemy experience permanent disgrace, in the name of Jesus.

11. Every power of darkness fuelling my problem, be arrested in the name of Jesus.

12. Thou fountain of problem in my life, dry up in the name of Jesus.

13. Every anointing of serpent in my life, dry up, in the name of Jesus.

14. I destroy the legal hold of the enemy upon my life, in the name of Jesus.

15. Evil storm of life, be still in the name of Jesus.

16. Powers assign to turn me to mincemeat in the market place of darkness, expire in the name of Jesus.

17. Every load of tragedy prepared for me in the spirit, catch fire and roast to ashes, in the name of Jesus.

18.O Lord, give me spirit of boldness to hold situation positive and straight, in the name of Jesus.

19.O Lord, give me the spirit of boldness to destroy works of darkness, in the name of Jesus.

20.O Lord, give me power over my enemy and subdue them, in the name of Jesus.

21.O Lord, give me miracle I can't comprehend, in the name of Jesus.

22.O Lord, give me spirit of Daniel, in the name of Jesus.

23.O Lord, paralyze my enemy and make them empty, in the name of Jesus.

24.O Lord, show love to me and my family, in the name of Jesus.

25.O Lord, give me spirit of love God and love my neighbor as myself, in the name of Jesus.

26.O Lord, move me from my position to mountain top in the name of Jesus.

27. O Lord, reverse bad situation that face me, in the name of Jesus.

28. I am not a candidate of Satan, the Lord Abba, is my father, he identify Himself with me.

29. O Lord, provide for me, you are Jehovah-Jireh, Provider of good things of life.

30. O Lord, let peace reign in my life, you are Jehovah Shallom, the Lord is peace.

31. O Lord, you are the Great Healer, heal every wound in my heart, in the name of Jesus.

32. No sickness or disease shall take over my life, in the name of Jesus.

33. My Father and my God, deliver me from evil and protect me from enemy, in the name of Jesus.

34. My God is El-Shaddai, the All-Powerful God, protect me, and be with me, in the name of Jesus.

35. O Lord my father see me through in all my endeavor, in the name of Jesus.

CHAPTER 7

MY GOD SHALL HONOUR ME

"He shall call upon me, and I will answer him: I will be with him in trouble; I will deliver him, and honour him. With long life will I satisfy him, and shew him my salvation." Psalm 91:15-16

The Lord promised six things here, if you call upon him. This means you must register your presence before God. The Lord says:-

1. He will answer you.

2. He will be with you in time of trouble.

3. He will deliver you.

4. He will honor you.

5. He will give you long life, and,

6. He will show you salvation.

Note this, you don't come to his presence and start talking or pray. Tell God your name, your gender and address if possible! Why?, because you are before Him to open register of prayer. Then God shall say, my son, my daughter, you are welcome.

The promise of God is a spiritual asset that gives peace of mind. God is ready for everyone who is ready to be on the same page with him. This is a rear bargain you must key into when you pray to God. He will answer you and your life shall change. Your barn will not empty. Mockers shall not near you. Healing shall be your daily asset. Heaven shall open unto you. When God answers you, laughter and joy shall be your portion. Your marriage shall be blessed, your home shall be peaceful; your children shall be a source of joy to you. They shall sit around the table with you. When God answers you, spiritual and physical robbers shall not come near you. Demonic neighbors shall be silenced. You shall plant and reap bountifully, because God answers you.

There is no problem or trouble that is too big for God to solve. There is no trouble bigger than God to fold his hands and say, "This is too much, how will I go about it" No trouble can make God fear on his throne. "I will be with him in trouble" means, in any situation or circumstance you think is negative, he will be with you. We are prayer less in small things that befall us as human being and at times we don't pray at all. We complain, this is too much, how will I go about it? When God promised He will be with us in time of trouble. We doubt and lose hope. But God says, he will be with you, have courage and look unto him. Because you go to God he will be with you and answer you in time of trouble.

The Lord says, "I will deliver him", whatever challenge you face, the Lord says he will deliver you. Look at Job, he lost virtually everything, when God delivered him, it was replaced in multiple. If it were other people he will complain and never seek the face of God. The situation shocked Job, but he refused to curse God. He did not deep hands into occult or rituals. He did not turn his back at God. And God answered him.

Job was honored. When God honored him, everybody around heard of it and praised God even to this generation. It may be this verse referred to Job. Job was honored, in wealth, in children, in property, in faith and in good health. In everything that will make one laugh and dance his dance, Job was honored with it. I pray that you shall be honored in Jesus name. Amen

The Lord promised us with long life. God back it up with the promise of you will not die untimely death. God says, I give you everything, you will enjoy it. Your labor will not be in vain. You will not build for others to take over as a result of sudden death. You shall not be a parent that have children but couldn't sponsor them as a result of poverty. When you have long life, knowledge and wisdom, you will apply it and make sure your investment does not fail. I pray your balance sheet shall favor you. If you apply accounting ratio, it will be positive. The ratio of your asset shall be high, the ratio of your income shall be high, your Return on Investment shall be positive because you supervise your investment with wisdom in good health, even at old age. As you do this, you will not bury your children, because your household is under the shadow of God in the secret place of God. The wing of God shall carry the family up because you are the shepherd of the house that doesn't lay hands on bad thing. You will all grow together. Danger will not visit your house. This is long life. It will go to your investment as well. Your investment and career will not crumble. When you have chains of business, it shall live long. Long life entails your source of income, because if you have long life without money, you will be dejected.

Salvation means being with God that your soul is safe. When your soul is safe, heaven is the answer after death. This means shall shout a shout of joy of, "I made it at last" You will receive crown of glory, crown of favor and mercy, crown of victory, crown of secret place of God! Salvation of God will not elude you, in the name of Jesus. Amen.

PRAYER POINTS

1. O Lord, I thank you for your mercy and favour upon me, in the name of Jesus.

2. O Lord, I thank you for being with me in time of trouble, in the name of Jesus.

3. O Lord, deliver me from the grip of poverty, in the name of Jesus.

4. O Lord, deliver me from power of darkness, in the name of Jesus.

5. O Lord, deliver my soul from pit of hell that enemy plan for me, in the name of Jesus.

6. O Lord, honor me among my peers in the name of Jesus.

7. O Lord, honor me wherever I go in the name of Jesus.

8. O Lord, give me honor of breakthrough and promotion in the name of Jesus.

9. O Lord, give me long life to worship you in the name of Jesus.

10. All ancient doors that hindered God's plan for me, break, in the name of Jesus.

11. O Lord, upgrade my brains and baptize me with wisdom and knowledge, in the name of Jesus.

12. Every spirit behind my problem expire, in the name of Jesus.

13. Every mocker around me, be silenced in the name of Jesus.

14. O Lord, bring joy and laughter to my family in the name of Jesus.

15. Any power assigned to empty my destiny, expire, in the name of Jesus.

16. O Lord my father, bless my marriage, in the name of Jesus.

17. O Lord, let my children, spouse and siblings be a source of joy to me in the name of Jesus.

18. I shall live long and see my children, children in the name of Jesus.

19. Every spiritual and physical robber be exposed and be disgraced in the name of Jesus.

20. Every power assign to oppress me, paralyze in the name of Jesus.

21. O Lord, let my portion come from your throne, in the name of Jesus.

22. Every obstacle in my life, give way to miracles, in the name of Jesus.

23. O God arise, speak healing with creative miracles to my life, in the name of Jesus.

24. Signs and wonders appear in my life, in the name of Jesus.

25. O Lord, let my stubborn problem be buried, in the name of Jesus.

26. Rod of the wicked attacking my progress, break, in the name of Jesus.

27. My enemies shall not rejoice over me in the name of Jesus.

28. Any power assign to sink the boat of my salvation, paralyze, in the name of Jesus.

29. O Lord my Father; deliver me from costly mistakes, in the name of Jesus.

30. O Lord, let me be celebrated, in the name of Jesus.

31. O Lord; support me, let my shame expire in the name of Jesus.

32. My glory, arise from the graveyard of backwardness and shine in the name of Jesus.

33. Owner of witchcraft load, carry your load, in the name of Jesus.

34. Shadow of blessings, rain of blessings, shall not seize in my life in the name of Jesus.

35. Evil clinical prophecy shall not come to pass in my life, in the name of Jesus.

36. O Lord, favor me now and forever more, in the name of Jesus.

37. I plug my destiny to socket of favor and breakthrough in the name of Jesus.

YOU HAVE BATTLES TO WIN
TRY THESE BOOKS

1. <u>COMMAND THE DAY: DAILY PRAYER BOOK</u>

Each day of the week is loaded with meanings and divine assurance. God did not create each day of the week for the fun of it. Blessings, success, gifts, resources, hopes, portfolios, duties, rights, prophecies, warnings and challenges, are loaded in each day.

Do you know the language, command or decree you can use to claim what belongs to you in each day of the week? Do you know in Christendom, Monday can be equated to one of the days of creation in Genesis chapter one? Do you know creation lasted for six days and God rested on the seventh day? What day of the week can Christian equate as the first day of the week, if we follow Christian calendar? What day can we call day seven?

This book shall give insight to these questions. It shall explain how you can command each day of the week according to creation in the book of Genesis chapter one.

Above all, you shall exercise your right and claim what is hidden in each day of the week.
Check for this in <u>COMMAND THE DAY: DAILY PRAYER BOOK</u>

2. <u>PRAYER TO REMEMBER DREAMS</u>

A lot of people are passing through this spiritual epidemic on a daily basis. Their dream life is epileptic, having no ability to remember all dreams they dream, or sometimes forget everything entirely. This is nothing but spiritual havoc you need to erase from your spiritual record.
The answer to every form of spiritual blackout

caused by spiritual erasers is found in, <u>PRAYER TO REMEMBER DREAMS</u>

3. <u>100% CONFESSIONS AND PROPHECIES TO LOCATE HELPERS AND HELPERS TO LOCATE YOU</u>

This is a wonderful book on confessions and prophecies to locate helpers and helpers to locate you. It is a prayer book loaded with over two thousand (2,000) prayer points.

The book unravels how to locate unknown helpers, prayers to arrest mind of helpers and prayers for manifestation after encounter with helpers.

4. ANOINTING FOR ELEVENTH HOUR HELP: HOPE AND HELP FOR YOUR TURBULENT TIMES

This book tells much of what to do at injury hour called eleventh hour. When you read and use this book as prescribed fear shall vanish in your life when pursuing a project, career or contract.

5. PRAYER TO LOCATE HELPERS AND HELPERS TO LOCATE YOU

Our divine helper is God. He created us to be together and be of help to one another. In the midst of no help we lost out, ending our journey in the wilderness.

There are keys assign to open right doors of life. You need right key to locate your helpers. Enough is enough; of suffering in silence.

With this book, you shall locate your helpers while your helpers shall locate you.

6. <u>FIRE FOR FIRE PART ONE: (PRAYER BOOK BOOK 1)</u>

This prayer book is fast at answering spiritual problems. It is a bulldozer prayer book, full of prayers all through. It is highly recommended for night vigil. Testimonies are pouring in daily from users of this book across the world!

7. <u>PRAYER FOR FRUIT OF THE WOMB: EXPECTING MOTHERS</u>

This prayer book is children magnet. By faith and believe in God Almighty, as soon as you use this book open doors to child bearing shall be yours. Amen

8. <u>PRAYER FOR PREGNANT WOMEN: WITH ALL CHRISTIAN NAMES AND MEANINGS</u>

This is a spiritual prayer book loaded with prayers of solution for pregnant women. As soon as you take in, the prayers you shall pray from day one of conception to the day of delivery are written in this book.

9. <u>WARFARE IN THE OFFICE: PRAYER TO SILENCE TOUGH TIMES IN OFFICE</u>

It is high time you pray prayers of power must change hands in office. Use this book and liberate yourself from every form of office yoke.

10. <u>MY MARRIAGE SHALL NOT BREAK: THE SECRET TO LOVE AND MARRIAGE THAT LASTS</u>

Marriage is corner piece of life, happiness and joy. You need to hold it tight and guide it from wicked intruders and destroyer of homes.

11. <u>VICTORY OVER SATANIC HOUSE PART ONE: RIDDING YOUR HOME OF SPIRITUAL DARKNESS</u>

Are you a tenant, Land lord bombarded left and right, front and back by wicked people around you?
With this book you shall be liberated from the hooks of the enemy.

12. <u>DICTIONARY OF DREAMS: THE DREAM INTERPRETATION</u>

DICTIONARY WITH SYMBOLS, SIGNS, AND MEANINGS

This is a must book for every home. It gives accurate details to about **10,000 (Ten thousand) dreams and interpretations,** written in alphabetical order for quick reference and easy digestion. The book portrays spiritual revelations with sound prophetic guidelines. It is loaded with Biblical references and violent prayers.
Ask for yours today.

For Further Enquiries Contact
THE AUTHOR
EVANGELIST TELLA OLAYERI
P.O. Box 1872 Shomolu Lagos.
Tel: 08023583168

FROM AUTHOR'S DESK

BEFORE YOU GO

Hello,

Thank you for purchasing this book. Would you consider posting a review about this book? In addition to providing feedback and arousing others into Christ's bosom, reviews can help other customers to know about the book.

Please take a minute to leave a review on this book.

I would appreciate that!

Thank you in advance, for your review and your patronage!!

If you would like to leave a review on my other books click the link below.

https://tellaolayeri.com/review.php

NOTE: You can get all my books from my website www.tellaolayeri.com

SHARE YOUR TESTIMONY

We love testimonies. We love to hear what God has done for you, your family, your business etc. as you draw close to Him in prayer. Please share your testimony with us.

https://tellaolayeri.com/testimony.php

NOTE: If you want your picture to be shown with your testimony send it to tellaolayeri@gmail.com

I also invite you to checkout our website at www.tellaolayeri.com and consider joining our newsletter (get free six powerful book) which we send out once in a while with great tips, testimonies and revelations from God's Word for a victorious living.

Feel free to drop us your prayer request. We will join faith with you and God's power will be released in your life and issue in question.

www.tellaolayeri.com/prayerrequest.php

GOOD NEWS!!!

My audiobook is now available, to get one visit **audible**.

If you are reading from my paperback visit **acx.com** and search **"Tella Olayeri."**

Brethren, to be loaded and reloaded visit: *amazon.com/author/tellaolayeri* for a full spiritual sojourn for my books.

Thanks.

DONATE TO THE MINISTRY

Why Give?

We have two major area of focus: The less Privileged and Charity.

Service to people and help to set up outstanding Modern Printing Press to reach thousands for free evangelism pamphlets and books to hinterland and the needy.

To achieve this, financial support is needed and we count you as one to support this ministry. A drop of water makes an ocean.

No donation is small or little. Donate through any of the ways listed below. May God bless your purse and source. Amen.

DONATE IN NAIRA

Bank Name: Guaranty Trust Bank Plc.

Account Name: OLAYERI ADIKU TELLA

Account Number: 0499255414

DONATE IN DOLLARS

Bank Name: Guaranty Trust Bank Plc.

Account Name: OLAYERI ADIKU TELLA

Account Number: 0499255098

Swift code: GTBINGLA

Visit the donation page on my website to donate online:

www.tellaolayeri.com/donate.php

ABOUT THE AUTHOR

Tella Olayeri grew from Spiritual Warrior to Spiritual Warlord in the Vineyard of God. His books have changed lives of millions, with banner of praises and testimonies in their hands!

He is a solution giver to problems and challenges men and women pass through on daily basis. He frowns at satanic oppression and demonic agenda propagated by powers of darkness. He is known for his wonderful deliverance books that address, swallow and bring abrupt end to fierce attacks of the enemy. **"Wonders and miracles"**, connotes his deliverance books.

Tella's books are globally read and accepted, based on operation "do-it-yourself". His books are instant solution to problems laced with fire prayer missiles that give instant deliverance to demonic yoke and oppression, health hazards, witchcraft attacks etc. His books will teach your hands to wage war and your fingers to fight against forces of darkness.

Tella Olayeri is a role model in Christian warfare. He is a Counselor and Preacher of the Word. His writings are wonderful and courageous for Christian soldiers in the battle of life to harvest breakthrough, salvation, spiritual protection, open doors and miracles.

One of his major research book is **DICTIONARY OF DREAMS**, that gives instant relief to millions of how to interpret dreams. The book has about ten thousand (10,000) dreams with accurate interpretations.

Tella Olayeri is happily married to his wife, Sister Ngozi Judith Olayeri. The marriage is blessed with five children, Miss Ibukun, David, Michael, Miss Comfort and Miss Mercy.

Connect with Tella Olayeri at www.tellaolayeri.com to receive powerful daily message.

www.ingramcontent.com/pod-product-compliance
Lightning Source LLC
Chambersburg PA
CBHW072053150726
47999CB00005B/1765